CHANGE _Almost_ ANYTHING IN 21 DAYS

Recharge Your Life with the Power of over 400 Affirmations

Ruth Fishel

Illustrated by Bonny Van de Kamp

Published by

Spirithaven

Marstons Mills, Cape Cod

Massachusetts

D0723396

Editor: Sandy Bierig

To the spirit of peace and love
in the universe.
May it find us all.

Change Almost Anything

TABLE OF CONTENTS

With Gratitude

This book would not have been possible without the help of so many people. It is with deep gratitude that I thank Sandy Bierig for her tireless editing, suggestions, encouragement, support and contributions.

It has been a joy to work with the very gifted Bonny Van de Kamp again. Bonny has been an important part of many of my books, dating back to 1987 with my first book *The Journey Within*.

Thank you, artist Nicki Garner, for your patience with me as I struggled to learn how to apply color in the cover. You did a wonderful job!

And, again I thank you, artists Gail O'Connell-Bierig and Brian Bierig, for always being willing to take time out of your busy schedule to instruct and support my projects.

I am so grateful all the time Jane Brown took to read, edit and make wonderful suggestions. You're a great teacher, Jane!

Thanks to my daughter, Debbie Boisseau and my good friend, Barbara Thomas, for all your helpful suggestions.

I'm very grateful to Dorna Allen, Karen Beaton, Mary Jane Beach, Lisa Boone , Leslie

Fabian, Mersh Lubel Kanis, Mindy Ruch, and Diane Webster and for contributing their special affirmations and sharing their powerful experiences.

There have been so many wonderful teachers I've had over the years including every client, retreat and workshop attendee. I can not name them all but you will always be in my heart and my gratitude.

And a special thank you to Bill W. and Dr. Bob without whom I would not be alive.

INTRODUCTION

*It takes only one person to
change your life...you.*
Ruth Casey

Dear Reader,

Are there parts of your life you would like to change? Are there places you would like to go? Things you would like to do? Have you been looking for a purpose in your life? Do you sometimes wonder why some people seem to get all the breaks when you get very few or none at all? Does life ever seem like an ongoing struggle? How many times have you wanted something to happen in your life and it didn't? Or even if almost everything is going just the way you want, is there something you would like to add or subtract from your life?

If you can say yes to any of these questions, there's a very good chance that this book can help you. I say, *can* help you, not, will help you, because whether it does or doesn't is up to you! The techniques in this book definitely *can* help you. But you have to be willing to change. Or at least be willing to be willing to change. Do you really want to let go of the old ways that haven't worked to find the courage to try new ones?

We can't always get what we want. Life just doesn't work that way. And, what we want is not always the best for us. But by making only one difference in your life, your life *can* get better. You *can* have more of what you want. You *can l*et go of some of your struggle. The question is, are you willing to put your energy and commitment into making a change?

As soon as you become willing to try the simple techniques in this book, incredible transformations will begin to happen in your life. You will quickly see the power and the possibilities that lie ahead of you.

I've seen people find new jobs, homes, cars, careers, hidden talents, attitudes, friendships and relationships. I've witnessed others experience remarkable results including healing from major illnesses, and no longer needing medication for diabetes and Attention Deficit Disorder. Addicts have become clean and sober, stopped smoking, given up gambling and over-spending. Students have passed exams they were sure they would fail. Fights have been avoided. Resentments have been healed. And many, many people have found peace of mind, improved their self-esteem, and made a deeper spiritual connection and a more meaningful purpose in their lives.

So go for it! Have some fun with this book and make changes that will add quality, serenity, happiness and joy to your life. You're worth it!

With love and peace,

Ruth Fishel
Cape Cod, 2001

CHANGE *Almost* ANYTHING IN 21 DAYS

Transformation is a journey
without a final destination.
    Marilyn Ferguson

Many years ago, while I was struggling to end my addiction to alcohol, a very wise man told me that we can change almost anything we want to change in our lives. He said we can change our name, our location, our careers, our relationships, just about everything, for one day. He said that most things could be changed back, if we didn't like the change. That was easy enough to say, but my struggle continued. How, I wondered, would change happen for me?

When I was a child my father instilled deeply in me the message that "Ruth could do anything." Over and over again, he repeated the story about how I had taught myself to ski. He told and retold it to anyone who would listen about how every time I fell down, I would pick myself up and start over. He said that was how I could do anything I wanted to do. Stay with the task I wanted to accomplish, and if I fell, simply pick myself up and start over again. Because of hearing of this message over and over again for so many years, I thought I really could do just about anything. But, that was until the compulsion to drink became stronger than I truly could handle and I couldn't stop, no matter how I tried.

Finally, with the help of many other recovering alcoholics, I was introduced to the concept of a Power Greater than myself. This was extraordinarily difficult for me at first because I was such an extremely independent and arrogant person and believed that God was simply a crutch used by very weak people. Believe in God if you want to, I thought, but not me! That's not what I need! However, nothing else was working. I simply could not stop drinking. Finally, after much pain and despair, I turned to this Power and humbly asked for help. The miracle happened. I soon lost my desire to drink.

I came to believe in a Power in the universe that I could not see or touch. I knew for certain

It was there. I saw It at work in the miracle of the changing seasons, the birth of my children, a seed becoming a flower. I saw the results in the changes in other peoples lives. Today I call that Power God.

Hungry to learn more, I went on to study about the power of prayer and meditation, intentions, and the power of words. I learned about the wonderful concept of the power of affirmations and the power of 21 days. Marvelous things began to happen. I became more confident. I overcame my fear of public speaking. I was able to help in the opening of an alcoholism treatment program for women when all odds were against us. My life began to change as I developed my ability to use these powerful techniques.

I also learned that it is not possible to change everything. There are some things, like winning the Olympics at the age of 62 or becoming an opera singer if you are tone deaf that are out of the realm of our ability to alter, no matter what we do, and we learn to accept limitations with time and experience. However, as we grow in our practice and become more open to allowing these powers to work in our lives, we discover that even if we wish for one result, it might not be in our best interests to have it. Something better might be waiting for us. We learn to trust the process of growth and change.

Eventually, I began teaching and writing about these subjects, because they work! My intention in writing this particular book is to take everything I know about affirmations, everything that I have learned from teachers, clients, workshop and retreat participants, friends and my own experience, and put it all in one place. This book is meant to be a vehicle for transformation. Anyone can pick it up and find the subject they wish to change and learn how to make it happen. After many years of teaching affirmations and utilizing them in my own life, I have found that one of the greatest barriers to successful outcomes is that people have difficulty wording affirmations to achieve the results they want.

What is unique in *Change (Almost) Anything in 21 Days* is that there are over 400 affirmations alphabetized according to topic. You can go to the index, and find a positive, powerful affirmation for almost any subject you want or need to change. For example, if you're nervous about a job interview or an upcoming exam, simply look up *fear* or *confidence* in the index. Do you want to lose weight? Check out *food* or a*ddiction*. If the affirmation you find doesn't feel quite perfect, rewrite it in your own words, remembering to use the five rules for successful affirmations discussed later in this book.

Experiment with affirmations. Experience their magnetism as they connect you with the power and energy of the universe. Know there is a power for good and love in the universe and watch how it can bring miraculous changes into your life!

INTENTIONS

Intentions set into process
every aspect of your life.
                    Gary Zukav

   Change begins with the intention to change. In the Seat of the Soul, Gary Zukav gives us the following example of intending to change your job. "As the intention to leave your present job emerges into your consciousness, you begin to open yourself up to the possibility of working somewhere else or doing something else. You begin to feel less and less at home with what your are doing. Your higher self has begun the search for your next job."

   I remember a time when I was looking for a new convertible. While I was in college I had a very old convertible. As my finances improved, I was able to get newer cars and finally could afford a new car. This was around the time that the Mustang and the Firebird convertibles first came out. I had not been aware of them until someone told me they were great cars. As I drove around town I began seeing them everywhere.

My children were very young and when we went on errands they would yell out, "There's a Firebird!" and "There's a Mustang!" I had created an intention and my awareness grew. It was as if the universe were providing me with plenty of opportunities to make a decision.

Volition is the mental urge or signal which precedes an action.
                                    Joseph Goldstein

So we begin with an intention. Something we want to add, reduce, change or let go. We *intend* to make it happen. And, with the following steps, we learn we can make the change.

SELF-TALK

*Thoughts of your mind have made
you what you are and thoughts of your
mind will make you what you become
from this day forward.*
                    Catherine Ponder

Before going any further into affirmations, it's important to take some time to become familiar with the term "self-talk." I use this term to describe the conversations we have in our minds, the things we say to ourselves and then believe. We constantly tell ourselves all kinds of things which we then internalize as truth. For example, a person with an eating problem might be 5' 4" tall and weigh 105 pounds and still tell herself she is too fat. A very competent person might not go for a job interview after convincing him or herself that he or she could not be hired.

It is crucially important to become aware of your self-talk if you hope to change it. Practice listening to the way you speak to yourself. Observe the effect that it has on your personal belief system..

Meditation is a wonderful technique for helping you to slow down and listen to your own thoughts. The practice of mindfulness, a form of meditation, not only helps you to increase your awareness of how you talk to yourself, but also helps you to stay in the present moment. I've written more about this in my books *The Journey Within, Precious Solitude and Stop! Do You Know You're Breathing?*

Mindfulness is simply a quieting down of our mind, a settling down of our thoughts. Sitting quietly for only 20 minutes every morning you begin to see how your mind works. By concentrating on your breathing, you'll see how your mind goes off in many other directions. Bring your attention back to your breathing. Every time your mind strays away, just notice it without any judgement and bring your attention back to your breathing.

This practice helps you become aware of your self-talk. People who are just beginning this practice are often amazed at the language they use on themselves. They might discover themselves using abusive language such as, "Stupid! I should be able to stay with my breath." Some people have been talking to themselves like this for their entire lives and have not been aware of it. They didn't know that they are holding themselves back or keeping themselves in a state of low self-esteem.

Once we recognize and understand the power our thoughts have over our actions and feelings, we can learn to detach emotionally from them and observe them, sorting out the negative and destructive ones from the positive and constructive ones; realizing we do not have to believe them. These thoughts lose their power over us as soon as we become aware of them because we can then choose to create more positive and constructive self-talk to inspire, encourage, affirm, accept, respect and love ourselves.

Remember:

> *We are what we think about!*
> *What we think about expands.*
> *We feel what we think about.*
> *We create what we think about in our*
>   *lives.*
> *When awareness increases, we draw to*
>   *us what we think about.*
> *We attract what we think about.*

THE POWER OF WORDS

*The word is not just a sound or a written
symbol. The word is a force, it is the
power you have to express and
communicate, to think, and thereby
to create the events of your life.*
                              Don Miguel Ruiz

Words are wonderful! They can lift your spirits, inspire you, change your mood, give you courage, make you cry, and much more. They can move your life forward. As you become aware of your self-talk, the words that you say to yourself, you can be mindful of the effect words have in your life. You will see how your mood can be changed by how you speak to yourself, thus creating changes in the quality of your life.

Our bodies do not know the difference between something real or something imagined. Our bodies respond to what we think about as if it were real. For example, think for a minute about something that makes you smile, or feel gentle or happy such as a puppy, an ice cream cone or a sunset. Notice how these images make you feel. Now think about a time when you were fearful, and notice how those thoughts make you feel. Nothing will be changed in reality, but you will suddenly feel different. Words can block us from success, or bring us success.

Change the thought, change the feeling, change the action.

Fear, for example, is only a thought triggering a physical sensation.

Your word can create the most beautiful dream, or your word can destroy everything around you.
Don Miquel Ruiz

Negative words blockers that keep us from moving forward:

When I say, "I can't," then I can't. I'll feel inadequate.

When I say, "I'll never be able to_____," then I never will be able to_____. I'll feel incapable.

When I say, "I haven't enough time," then I'm all about not having enough time. I'll feel rushed and full of anxiety.

Positive word releasers

When I say, "I AM TERRIFIC JUST THE WAY I AM!" I feel energized, enthused, upbeat.

When I say, "I am feeling peace in this very moment," I feel serene and peaceful.

When I say, "I have all the intelligence I need to pass this test," I feel confident and strong.

POWER OF AFFIRMATIONS

*What we create within is mirrored outside
of us. That is the law of the universe.*
Shakti Gawain

When my first book *The Journey Within: A
Spiritual Path to Recovery,* was printed, Peter,
my publisher, called to ask if I did public speaking. I said no. He asked if I would consider it
and I said no. He asked me to call him back in
two weeks. I didn't. I was terrified of public
speaking. I had some very embarrassing moments in school as a child and vowed I would
never speak in front of people again. Peter called
back in three weeks and told me I was on the
agenda to speak in Albany, New York in Octo-
ber, three months away. I felt trapped and I had
three long months in front of me to feel my ter-
ror!

After listening to my negative self-talk, such
as "I'm not good enough," and "Who would want
to hear me speak?" for over two months, I remembered, fortunately, that affirmations work.

I had been teaching affirmations in my meditation classes, yet my own fear blocked me from remembering to use them in this instance.

One important criteria for successful affirmations is to write each affirmation ten times a day for twenty-one consecutive days. By the time I remembered to use affirmations it was only nineteen days before the conference. Could it work with in the time left? I wrote the following affirmation ten times a day for nineteen days, hoping there would be enough time:

I am a dynamite, confident, fearless, charismatic and motivating speaker.

I didn't believe one word of it and was embarrassed to tell anyone my affirmation, but the power of those words carried me through that speaking engagement and hundreds of others since then. I soon became relaxed when speaking before an audience and now even enjoy it.

I've learned that the more we learn to quiet our minds and listen to our self-talk, the more we begin to discover that words have the power to make us feel good or bad, confident or fearful, positive or negative. It has been scientifically proven that the words we use can even make us healthy or sick.

Brain wave tests show that endorphins, our positive "feel good" hormones, flow when we use positive words. They stop flowing when we use negative words.

We will have a new and extraordinarily effective technique for change when we realize that the way we feel can be a direct result of how we talk to ourselves. We do have a choice.

Affirmations are powerful tools for helping us break away from the way we normally think and talk to ourselves. By changing our thinking we can change our attitude. By changing our attitude we can change our energy. And by changing our energy we can change our actions and thus we change our lives.

Affirmations are so easy that some people think they are too simple to be effective. I have used them over and over and have taught them to thousands of people and the results have been amazing.

WHAT IS AN AFFIRMATION?

Whether you think you can or can't,
you're right!
                    Henry Ford

Affirmations are positive statements we say to ourselves. The definition of the word affirm, in Funk & Wagnalls Standard College Dictionary is "to declare or state positively; assert and maintain to be true."

Five Parts to a Successful Affirmation

In order for an affirmation to be effective it must have each of the following characteristics. They must be:

1. **POSITIVE**
   We say, "I am confident today," not, "I am no longer negative."
2. Said and felt with **PASSION** and **POWER**
   We say, "I am *confident* today!" with feeling and enthusiasm.
3. Be in the **PRESENT** moment

We say, "I am confident TODAY," not,
"I will be confident."

4. **POSSIBLE**

   I cannot affirm that I am a famous singer,
   as I am tone deaf; but I can affirm that I
   am a successful writer.

5. **PERSONAL**

   We can not affirm for someone else, only
   for ourselves.

**Write Your Affirmation 10 Times a Day for
21 Consecutive Days.**

Once you have created an affirmation or cho-
sen one that fits you from the affirmation index,
you now must write it 10 times a day for 21 *consecutive* days. This is a critical component for
success. Writing uses more of your senses. You
can *feel, see* and *smell* the pen and the paper or
the computer as you write the affirmation. You
can *hear* your voice as you say the affirmation
out loud or to yourself as you write. You are
imprinting your affirmation deeply into your
mind and your body.

Why 21 Days?

Many years ago I read *Psycho-Cybernetics* by Maxwell Maltz. Dr. Maltz was a plastic surgeon who operated primarily on faces. He noticed, he said, a sudden and dramatic change in personality in most cases when he operated on "a person who had a conspicuously ugly face, or some 'freakish' feature. Usually there was a rise in self-esteem and self-confidence in 21 days. Those who didn't change continued to feel just as if they still had an ugly face."

Dr. Maltz wrote that it usually requires 21 days to effect any perceptible change, and he suggests reserving all judgement for 21 days. When an arm or a leg is amputated, the "phantom limb" persists for about 21 days. Though no one knows exactly why this number holds such power over mind and body, Dr. Maltz and others have observed this phenomena.

When I began practicing affirmations I remembered what Dr. Maltz wrote about 21 days and I began to apply his observation. I remember the time that I was involved in starting a halfway house for women recovering from alcoholism. We desperately wanted to find the right house, raise the money, get the town to approve, get a contract with the state, and so on. Finally, after a tremendous effort on the part of a great many people, we accomplished enough of our goals to move into the halfway house. I could not understand why I wasn't thrilled. I felt down, inexplicably, as if there were something very wrong. It took me about three weeks to feel at home and enjoy the hard-won accomplishment. Right on target, according to Dr. Maltz.

21 Days Means 21 Consecutive Days

We often begin a new project with great enthusiasm and energy. Perhaps we buy a new notebook and place it just where we can see it every day. Or we might carry it with us so we won't forget about our commitment.

Then the energy begins to wane, the enthusiasm begins to slip away. This usually happens for me around the sixth or seven day. My fingers begin to cramp before I even finish writing. My self-talk begins such as "is this really going to work?" Am I holding my pen too tightly? I flex my fingers. 21 days now seem so long! I start thinking that I really don't have enough time and I'll write the affirmation later.

Soon I forget and I miss a day and need to

start over. And then, maybe after only two or three days, I miss another one and I have to start over again. Once it took me six months to finish writing, "God is guiding the perfect person to us to buy our house today" ten times a day for 21 consecutive days. A purchase and sale agreement was signed just a few days after I finally completed 21 consecutive days.

SUGGESTIONS FOR SUCCESSFUL AFFIRMATIONS
Simple Steps for Change

Create your Intention.

Decide what you would like to change.

Create your affirmation.

Choose from over 400 affirmations in this book or write your own.

Visualize the results.

Don't wait for your intention to come true. Don't even wait until you believe it will come true. Visualize it *now* as if it were true in the present moment.

Keep a separate notebook.

Use it only for your affirmations. Keep this notebook in the same place all the time. If you are a daily meditator, it is a good idea to keep it where you meditate. Then you can get into a routine and do one routine after the other. Keeping the notebook on a table next to your bed will help you remember when you wake up or before you go to sleep.

I've found that when I use the notebook that includes other things as well, such as my "to do" list or other writing ideas, it can end up on my desk in another room, or in a bag I carry to teach meditation or put on a workshop. I have skipped many a day because the book wasn't where I could see it to remind me to write, causing me to start over again and again. When the notebook is next to my bed in clear view, I don't miss a day.

Use your computer.

It's okay to type affirmations into your computer as long as you actually type the sentences out 10 times each day. This can save your fingers from cramping. You will also know that you have your affirmation saved in one place.

Dittos don't count!

Use Reminders

If you are writing your affirmation in your computer, it's helpful to place a sticky note right on the frame of your monitor so you will see it every day. It also helps to write your affirmation as soon as you sit down at your computer, because if you do something else first, the note often blends into the furniture. You'll no longer be aware of it and you might miss the day and have to start over again. Your computer calendar can also be set to pop up every day to remind you to write your affirmation.

Remember, the affirmation needs to be written for 21 *consecutive* days. Therefore do anything you can to help you remember to write it. You can place a reminder on your bathroom mirror, on a file card for your purse or pocket, on the visor of your car or on your refrigerator.

Begin with gratitude.

It is a good idea to list some things you are grateful for before beginning a new affirmation. As Sharon Anderson writes in *The Universal Spiritual Laws*: "If you're not grateful for what you already have, why should the Universe give you more?"

Use one primary affirmation at a time.

I am often asked if it is all right to write more than one affirmation at a time. Yes, you can. But, choose one to be your primary affirmation. This way, if you are unable to continue writing more than one, you can maintain the most important one until the 21 days are completed. Later, you can go on to do another one.

Listen your self-talk.

As you go through your day, notice that negative, limiting thoughts are in direct or indirect opposition to reaching your goal. It can be as direct as "I'll never make it. I'm not smart enough," or so indirect that you can barely notice it such as "Now *there's* a smart *dresser*!" In this case you might not be aware that you're really putting yourself down.

Become aware of your judgements.

Notice your likes, dislikes and opinions. Don't judge yourself for having them. Simply raise your awareness of them.

Write down your limiting thoughts.

Take some time to write down the blocks that keep you stuck. As you listen to your self-talk and watch your negative thinking, write everything all down without any judgement. Accept them as a part of you, not all of you.

The more you become tuned into the thoughts
that keep you stuck, the more quickly
you will be able to let them go.

Begin to connect your thoughts to your feelings
Notice how positive thoughts connect with pleasant feelings while negative thoughts make you feel tense, angry, unhappy or depressed. You will soon increase your ability to be aware of how your thoughts affect your moods and your actions. You will see how these words have the power to make you feel good or bad, confident or fearful, positive or negative. It has been scientifically proven that the words we tell ourselves can heal us or make us sick. It has also been scientifically proven that positive words increase the flow of our endorphins, our feel-good hormones, thus making us feel better. Negative thoughts block our endorphins and that can lead to depression.

Change how you talk to yourself.
Once we realize that the way we feel is a direct result of how we talk to ourselves, then we have a new and powerful tool to change our feelings. We have a choice.

There's a wonderful Sioux Indian story about how our thoughts not only create our own feelings but affect the feelings of others. "My grandfather took me to the fish pond on the farm when I was about seven, and he told me to throw a stone into the water. He told me to watch the circles created by the stone. Then he asked me to think of myself as that stone person."You may create lots of splashes in your life but the waves that come from those splashes will disturb the peace of all your fellow creatures," he said.

"Remember that you are responsible for what you put in your circle because that circle will also touch many other circles. You will need to live in a way that allows the good that comes from your circle to send the peace of that goodness to others. The splash that comes from anger or jealousy will also send those feelings to other circles. You are responsible for both.

"That was the first time I realized each person creates the inner peace or discord that flows out into the world. We cannot create world peace if we are riddled with inner conflict, hatred, doubt or anger. We radiate the feelings and thoughts that we hold inside, whether we speak them or not. Whatever is splashing around inside of us is spilling out into the world, creating beauty or discord with all other circles of life. Remember the eternal wisdom: *whatever you focus on expands."*

Turn around your "I can't because..."

Soon you'll begin to know how your *I can't*s really hold you back. For example, change "I can't get into college because I'm not smart enough," to "I'm smart enough to get into just the right college for me." Change "I can't lose weight because I've tried it before and it never lasts," to "I'm moving toward the perfect weight for me today." You get the idea! Trust that the universe will provide you with the perfect college, the perfect weight, the perfect relationship. You simply need to provide the willingness and the intention to follow where it leads.

Take one step at a time.

Many years ago I attended EST, a personal training seminar. We were taught a simple lesson that has stayed with me over the years. The trainer asked us to turn and look at a door in the back of the room. He then stated an obvious fact, "No matter how much you want to be at that door, you can't just be at that door. You can only get there one step at a time."

Alcoholics Anonymous teaches the same message. Alcoholics don't have to imagine not drinking for the rest of their lives. They just have to stay sober one day at a time.

In this age of fast food, instant messages and wireless phones, we have come to expect everything to happen right now. We want success, fame, money and everything else immediately.

If we don't have instant gratification, we become frustrated and impatient.

You have to do the footwork
> *Knowledge without action is the*
> *greatest self-con of all.*
> *Sharon Wegscheider-Cruse*

Relationships can improve through changes in our attitude. Attitudes can improve by writing our affirmations 10 times a day consistently for 21 days. As long as we are willing to change and make an intention for it to occur, change will happen. Negative feelings can be released when we focus on positive affirmations, thus reducing and eliminating barriers between ourselves and others.

Still, we must realize that affirmations aren't magic. Our dreams aren't necessarily going to suddenly manifest into our lives just because we write them ten times a day for 21 days. Many affirmations require more effort on our parts. A new job won't come to us just because we have affirmed that we are getting one and then only stay home and watch TV. We might have to do research to find the appropriate companies, write a good resume, and perhaps, even buy a new outfit and go on job interviews.

If we want a new relationship we can't simply sit in our living rooms and wait for the phone or doorbell to ring. Although the person who delivers the mail might be just the person we want to be with for the rest of our lives, most likely we have to go to places where single people meet or join a group or club or organization.

Our affirmations create positive energy and help us to be open to positive change.

Father Martin gives us this wonderful example:

" There was a young woman who wanted to be a doctor. Every night she prayed and prayed that God would make her a doctor. After ten years of praying with nothing happening she asked God why He didn't help her become a doctor. And she heard a voice say, 'Go to medical school.'"

Another wonderful example is a Sufi story adapted by Anthony de Mello:

A man walked through the forest and saw a fox that had lost its legs and wondered how it lived. Then he saw a tiger come up with game in its mouth. The tiger ate its fill and left the rest of the meat for the fox.

The next day God fed the fox by means of the same tiger. The man began to wonder at God's greatness and said to himself, "I too shall just rest in the corner with full trust in the Lord and he will provide me with all that I need."

He did this for many days but nothing happened. He was almost at death's door when he heard a voice say, "Oh you who are on the path of error, open your eyes to the truth! Stop imitating the disabled fox and follow the example of the tiger."

We don't always get what we want.

Shakti Gawain, author of *Creative Visualizations*, wrote that when completing an affirmation, know or say, "this or something better for all concerned is manifesting itself for me." It is not always true that we know what is best for ourselves, and if we learn to wait and listen, the right answer will be there.

BARRIERS TO CHANGE

Fear

You might think that if you get the new job, you won't be capable of handling the responsibilities that come with it. Or perhaps you are afraid that the person who didn't get the job will feel discouraged, or, even worse, be upset with you. Fear has been described as:

> False
> Evidence
> Appearing
> Real

If you worry or have fear, you are not living in the present moment. You're in the future, creating a scenario straight from your imagination.

Self-limiting thoughts

Thoughts such as, "I'm not good enough," or "I'll never pass this exam," or "I'll never get that job," keep us from moving forward.

As I wrote earlier, I love convertibles. Ever since I was in college I've had a convertible. In my years without much money, my convertibles were old. Later, I was able to afford newer ones. The only time I did not have a convertible in my life was during the first ten years that I co-founded and co-directed Serenity, Inc., an alcoholism treatment program for women.

A small grant from the state covered only a portion of our expenses and in order to make ends meet we were dependent on outside donations. People who believed in our cause donated money, sometimes when they barely had enough money of their own. I remember a blind woman once saved $6.00 and donated it to us. Churches raised money through bake sales.

One of the fringe benefits in lieu of a decent salary was that I did get the use of a company car. I bought one of the least expensive cars on the market. My thoughts were that if I bought a convertible, people would think I was using donated money frivolously and would stop making donations. But, oh, how I longed for a convertible.

Thinking about this one day, I realized that I had never done an affirmation around having a convertible. People I knew were getting new jobs, new relationships and much more as I drove in a car that blocked me from the joy of feeling the breeze in my hair and the sun on my face. I decided I would write an affirmation. So I began,

"I deserve a convertible." I had only written for four days when a friend said she received a call from another friend who saw a convertible for sale in a parking lot near her home. As I rushed over to look at it, a light went on in my mind. It was a 1969 Mustang. The year this happened for me was 1986. The car was 17 years old. It was too new to be a classic or worth much money, but it had been well cared for by the people who loved it.

It had never occurred to me to be looking for an older convertible. My mind had been closed, stuck in the idea of "what would people think" if I drove around in a convertible. I assumed people would judge it to be a flashy, extravagant and expensive car.

I called the number printed on the windshield and was delighted to hear that the price was only $3100.00; and yes, I could have the car checked out by my mechanic. In a few days I felt as if I were in heaven, driving guilt free, one with the wind and sun, in a car I paid for by myself.

My old "what would people think" tapes had kept me from something that gave me a great deal of enjoyment. My self-talk produced the fear that if people didn't approve of what I was doing, they wouldn't give us any more donations.

Worry

If you play the same CD over and over again, you're going to hear the same music!
                                    R.F.

Worry is similar to fear. Worry thoughts go round and round in our minds, drain our energy and leave us depressed and uninspired. Affirmations are an excellent way to get rid of worry and fear thoughts.

Focusing on what you don't want

Our focus is often on thoughts such as not wanting to struggle, or be fat, or live alone and so forth. When we think of what we don't want, we are putting a negative message out into the universe. The universe hears struggle, stress, fat, or live alone, etc.

A good way to turn this around is to make a list of what you don't want and turn them around to your wants. For example, if you don't want to be fat, think *thin* instead. If you don't want to feel stress, think *relax.* If you don't want financial insecurity, think *prosperity.*

Not really being willing

I have lived with clutter in my office and wherever else I work ever since I can remember. Within a half hour into speaking at a conference or workshop, I can look down and see my papers scattered here and there. I recreate my work environment wherever I am! I remember as clearly as yesterday walking through Harvard Square in Cambridge, Massachusetts, the year after I graduated from college and seeing a plaque in a store window jump out at me: *Tomorrow I'm going to get organized!"*

Yes! I said to myself, and went into the store to buy the plaque. I have carried it with me everywhere I have moved since that day and have hung it in every office I have been in where I can easily see it.

I am actually very organized when it comes to a specific project I am working on, such as when I am writing a book or preparing for a workshop. My bills are all in one place, as are many of the other projects I might work on at one time or another. But there is still a large pile of paper scattered everywhere. Recently a friend suggested that I have been putting out the word *tomorrow* into the universe, rather than "I am getting organized today" or "I am an organized person." I might try that...tomorrow!

If you think you would like to make a change but still have hesitation about it, try affirming for the willingness to be willing to make the change and see what happens. If your hesitation lessens and your determination increases, begin a new affirmation creating the change. For example, I can affirm, "I'm willing to be willing to be more organized," or, "I'm willing to move toward being a more organized person." Then, when my willingness increases, I can affirm "I'm an organized person today!"

Monkey mind
Our minds have been compared to monkeys, jumping from branch to branch going where ever they want to go. Writing affirmations helps us to focus, to keep our mind where we want it to be and not jumping everywhere it wants to go.

If we don't let go, we can't move forward.
RF

If you are regretful about the past or worrying about the future, your energy is stuck and you can't move forward.

Thinking you have to do everything yourself

Whether you believe in God or not, know that there is more than we know. We didn't create the universe. A Power beyond us did. When we allow ourselves to open to universal energy, when we let a Higher Power be in charge of our lives, we can relax and go with the flow. And as we relax and give up our fears and doubts, our tension and resistance, change begins to take place. Miracles begin to happen. Life becomes so much easier.

GOALS AND DREAMS VS. LIVING IN THE NOW

It's important to know that you don't have to wait for the results of your affirmations to transpire before you can be happy. Many people think that they can only be happy when or if things change. They think, "If I could just block this pain I would be happy," or, "When I get a new job, my life will be better," or, "When I hit the lottery," or, "Move to Cape Cod," or, "Move away from Cape Cod," my life will be complete." Some of us think happiness lies outside of ourselves, when it really lies in within us.

This present moment leads us into the next moment and into the next moment. When we can stay in the present moment, life naturally moves us forward. This is the way of life. Spring moves into summer moves into fall moves into winter and moves into spring again. When we follow our inner spirit and let our soul direct our course, our lives flow.

What does "being fully alive in the present moment" mean? And how do we get there? Living in the present moment simply means being free to be with whatever is going on in your life now, without wishing it to be different. It means not letting yourself be blocked by feelings of anger, resentment, guilt or shame from the past or fears of the future. It means letting go of judgements and opinions and simply accepting what is right now... and right now... and right now.

It also means growth and change. Our natural inclination is to grow and change, wish and want. Human beings are constantly evolving. This seems to be in conflict with accepting what is right now. How can we evolve and still be in the now? And why use affirmations to change if we want to learn to be content and accept the moment?

While our intention is to find peace in the moment, to be okay in this moment, it does not mean that we have to stay in unhealthy, unpleasant conditions. For example: The job you are in might be very stressful or even abusive, so that you have decided to leave and find a new job. It might mean staying in your old job a bit longer because you can't afford to leave before you have the new job because you need your weekly salary. However, you can learn to be peaceful with your decision to leave. You can use affirmations such as "God is guiding me toward the perfect job for me" or, "I am discovering the perfect job for me today." We still can have our goals and dreams, but we don't need to reach them in order to feel peace and contentment. We can be content in the knowledge that we are moving toward them.

Perhaps our lives are positive and full and there isn't anything we want to change. We can still grow and learn while we are content and grateful for what we have in our lives.

There are so many things that block us from letting our soul direct our path. Here is where our affirmations can help. Affirmations take us by the hand and help us step over a barrier or climb over a wall or move away a rock or a stick. Affirmations make it possible to change the negative thinking that keep us stuck, to rewire the circuitry in our brain. Affirmations help us direct our thoughts to a Higher Power, giving the energy in the universe permission to flow through us. Affirmations help us to clarify our dreams, expand and raise our consciousness, and let our heart stretch open and fill with love.

LEARNING TO STAY IN THE
PRESENT MOMENT

You can't make anything happen if you're wasting your energy regretting the past or living in fear of the future. You can only move forward when you are focused in the present moment.

A good technique to help you become aware of how much you are in the past or in the future is to watch what happens to your mind when you are doing something routine like taking a shower or brushing your teeth. Notice how often you are into planning, thinking, regretting, daydreaming or worrying.

A great way to practice staying in the present moment is to take that time in the shower or brushing your teeth and bring your full awareness to all your senses that are involved:

Feel the water on your body or in your mouth.

Feel the texture of the soap or the toothbrush in your hand.

Listen to the sound of the toothbrush against your teeth and gums.

Hear the water as it pours from the faucet.

Smell the soap and the toothpaste.

Observe all the details of where you are and what you are doing.

WHEN NOT TO THINK ABOUT
MAKING CHANGES

There are times when it is not in our best interests even to consider changing anything. There are times when staying right where we are is exactly where we belong. Here are a few examples:

Grief

When we experience a loss of any kind whether it be from a job, friendship or death of a loved one, it is important that we don't hide from those feelings or feel as if we have to rush through them and move on. Some people try to bury the pain from loss by the use of drugs, alcohol, food or other stimulants such as gambling or shopping. Any kind of over-consuming may make you feel better for the moment, but sooner or later you will have to deal with the feelings if you are to remain healthy and eventually move your life forward.

There are many ways to move through grief. Talking about your feelings to a friend or therapist is one of the most helpful ways. Writing, when talking about them is too difficult or impossible, helps to keep the feelings from being stuck inside. Praying and meditating, taking time with nature and joining a support group all help to get through these difficult times.

Affirmations can help. Look in the index for **difficult situation, faith, grief** and **healing.**

Stuck in the past

There are times in our lives when we must stop and do some serious soul searching. Sometimes exploring our history is important. We can't go forward fully until we look at our past and make peace with it. We might need to let go of old anger and resentments. We can't move forward until we become willing to forgive ourselves and others. We have to give up alcohol or drugs or other addictions so we can be fully present in each moment. We must let go of feelings of victimization or self-pity.

Twelve Step Programs have a technique that can be used by anyone. They suggest taking a personal inventory of the exact nature of wrongs we have done to others and then talking about them to God and another human being. This process helps to release anger, resentments and any guilt and shame we might be holding on to from the past. Done faithfully, real life changes occur.

Look in the index for **acceptance, letting go** *or* **forgiveness.**

Healing

Sometimes we just need to stop and rest and heal, such as after an operation, or a huge disappointment.

Look in the index for **healing, health, meditation** or **miracles.**

Slowing down and resting

Perhaps you have just put a tremendous amount of energy in a massive project, such as studying for the bar exam or doing a science project. It might be time to simply slow down, rest, and take some time off before even thinking about moving forward.

Look in the index for **meditation, time** or **solitude.**

Time out

It's important to have balance in our lives. Take a vacation, go on a retreat or just do absolutely nothing! Stop and have fun!

Look in the index for **fun, peace** or **relaxation.**

YES, THEY WORK!

Over the years, many people have shared their successful experiences with affirmations with me. The following are a just few.

On weight

Karen send in this success story:

"At one time I weighed 194 pounds. I had read about affirmations, that the subconscious could not discern between truth or fiction and that whatever you told yourself, and believed, would be who you became. I had become an overweight woman. After all, I wasn't meant to be thin, according to an old family belief. I was thrilled to learn on the day that I read about affirmations that I could create new weight and body type affirmations to literally change and transform my body and my mind.

These are the affirmations I wrote:

I weigh 145 pounds and I always have enough time, energy and desire to exercise my body.

I weigh 145 pounds and I have created my perfect body with slim, trim limbs and firm toned muscle.

I weigh 145 pounds and I maintain my weight easily as I only eat foods that are healthy and consistent with a slim, trim figure.

Nothing tastes as good as thin feels.

It has worked for a long time. I weighed between 140 to 145 for fifteen years! I now weigh 160 and need to use my affirmations again."

House sale

My good friend Dorna wrote:

"Several years ago it was imperative that I sell my home. I put it on the market and waited. Time passed, but no one made an offer to buy, and I grew increasingly discouraged. Then my friend, Ruth, suggested that I create an affirmation to bring about the sale of my home. She said I needed to write this affirmation 10 times each day for 21 days, and by the end of this period, my home would be sold.

Although I held no belief in the power of this kind of validation, I decided to try it anyway, and began to write: "Today God is directing the perfect person to me to buy my home." I continued with my affirmation in spite of disbelief, and wrote daily as I had been told to do.

Time went by with no results, and I found

myself saying, "See, it's all foolishness. My house hasn't been sold. I knew this wouldn't work!" But I kept writing! On the 19th day of affirmation, I received offers from two buyers, and in a matter of weeks, my home was under contract. Today, I am a believer in the power of affirmation, and urge others with skepticism to witness the miracle and become believers, too!"

Negative thinking

Mindy, a woman with fourteen years sobriety, wrote that she had been having a terrible time with negative thinking when she was eleven years sober. Her sponsor taught her about affirmations, and they eventually changed her life. He told her to stand in front of the mirror, look into her eyes and tell herself, " I am a powerful woman. I am loving, kind, caring and giving; I can do anything I want to do; I am beautiful just the way I am."

"Did I believe them? " she wrote. "No, of course not. Then about one month later something started to happen. I started to believe what I was telling myself. They were working. This changed my whole life respecting self-esteem, self-respect and self-love. Unbelievable! It worked. Miracles began to happen, one day at a time."

Self-confidence

Mary Jane Beech, founder and director of Bridges Associates, Inc. in Hyannis, Massachusetts, a program for children with special needs and learning disabilities told me a wonderful tribute for affirmations. Ten years ago, a group of parents identified self-confidence as the most important factor influencing child success and began the "plant the seed of confidence campaign." They found that affirmations are the best ways to build self-confidence. Many children, parents and teachers report that they feel better using daily affirmations.

A time for every season

Sometimes no matter how much we would like to change something, the timing isn't always in our control. One woman told me the story of how she desperately wanted to be in a relationship. I suggested she write the affirmation: "God is guiding me into a healthy and loving relationship."

She went to a party a week later and met

someone she really liked, but didn't hear from that person for some time. Then, one year later, she received an invitation to dinner. The person she met a year ago had just not been ready yet, but kept her number, knowing that they would get together some day. They have been in a healthy and loving relationship ever since.

There are times when we set the energy into motion by our affirmation and think that it isn't working, when months later the job, house, or relationship might come through. And there are times when what we think is right for us just isn't meant to be. You will always get what you need at the right time. There's an old saying that God is never late.

Financial insecurity

Nan worked at a non-profit agency and could barely make ends meet on her $18,000 salary. She knew she was a very good therapist and had wanted to start her own private practice for years. Fear of financial insecurity held her back.

I suggested she try an affirmation. She was willing and wrote, "I am working for myself and earning $18,000 a year." I proposed she double that figure and she laughed and said that was an impossible figure. Within one year Nan was earning $38,000 and a few years later was earning over $50,000 and climbing.

Transforming stress into gratitude

Mersh has some favorite affirmations that she uses in times of stress. When she is having a particularly stressful moment, she stops what she's doing, especially if self-defeating reactions threaten to erupt. Then she silently reminds herself of one or more of her favorite affirmations or intentions, such as:

"I welcome the transformation and relief that a simple, intentional moment can bring.

I feel nothing but gratitude for the way in which using this positive power can turn the itchy discomfort of defeat and self-doubt into a welcoming wrap of love, care and possibility."

A few of her others include:

I am responsible, organized, motivated and productive today.

With every cleansing breath from the universe, I heal my body as I meditate today.

I am kind and gentle with myself and others today.

I make things easy on myself today.

Breaking a bad habit

When Nancy's daughter, Joan, was five years old, she began to pick at her fingers, making them very sore. Although she tried many things, such as scolding, painting the fingernails so they would look pretty, or putting on salve to help them heal, nothing worked.

Nancy followed a nightly ritual since Joan was a baby. She went into Joan's room after she was asleep to whisper soothing words and affirmations to her. Now she began to add the words "you are peaceful with the details of life" from Louise Hay's book "Heal Your Body." Within a week or two Joan stopped picking her fingers!

HOW TO USE THIS BOOK

Now you have read *how t*o use affirmations, when to use affirmations and *why* to use affirmations. Are you ready to *use* affirmations? Are you ready to make a change; add something to your life; let go of something in your life?

When you're ready to make a change, turn to the subject of your intentions and find an affirmation that feels good. If none feel right to you, write one of your own. Remember, you don't have to believe it. It is something you are going *toward*. You're *moving* in that direction.

Subjects are often interconnected. For example, if you're seeking to find more love in your life, you might look at **resentments**, to see what or who is filling your heart with anger or pain. Or look at **letting go**, to see what you are holding onto that is blocking you from feeling love. There's an old saying that if you have one foot in the past and one foot in the future, you can't be in the present moment.

Affirmations for losing weight can be found under **addiction, food** and **weight.** A new job affirmation can be found under **career** or **purpose.**

If you have the time, it would be wonderful if you could find a quiet place where you won't be interrupted. Sit quietly and meditate for 10 or 20 minutes. Meditation helps you to connect with God, Higher Power, Allah, Universal Energy or anything you want to call the Power that is greater than ourselves. You can connect with your angels, or spirit guides, whatever you believe works.

Find an affirmation that feels right for you or rephrase it in any way that makes you most comfortable. The affirmations in the index of this book are simply suggestions. Personalize them in any way you wish. Or write your own!

When you become willing to follow these simple instructions, incredible tranformations will begin to occur in your life.

Change Almost Anything

RECHARGE YOUR LIFE WITH THE POWER OF OVER 400 AFFIRMATIONS!

Let yourself *feeel* the power of these affirmations and discover how they can change the way you feel. Discover how they can change your life.

If we believe we are going to change, we are going to change!

ABUNDANCE

*Expect your every need to be met. Expect
the answer to every problem, expect
abundance on every level.*
Eileen Caddy

I have abundance in all areas
of my life.

I am open to all the blessings of
the universe.

I deserve to have wonderful
things happening to me.

I have everything I need today.

Everything I need is flowing into
my life today.

The Universe is providing me with

_____

(Add in your own intention or desire here).

I allow God to provide me with abundance on all levels.

ACCEPTANCE

I accept myself just as I am today.

I accept my limitations.

I am learning to accept limitations in myself and others.

I accept my progress today.

I accept others as they are today.

ADDICTIONS/ See Weight and Food also

I don't gotta even if I wanna.

I feel the joy of being a non-smoker.

It feels so good to be drug and alcohol free!

I am proud of my healthy eating today.

I am free from the desire to

_____

(Add your own word(s) here, i.e., over-eat, spend, gamble, work, control).

I am a sober person today.

I am drug-free today.

AGING

I am managing my aging process with grace and acceptance.

I am at the perfect age for me today!

ANGELS

My guardian angel is guiding me to my good today.

Unseen angels are looking after me today and all is well.

I await the encompassing love
of my guardian angel and know
that all is well in my life today.

With the help of all my angels
my life is changing in a positive
way today.

With the help of my angels, I
face any difficult situation and
come through easily and
effortlessly.

ANGER

Remember, every minute spent angry
is sixty seconds of happiness wasted.
Author Unknown

ANGER

I am learning to express my anger in healthy ways.

I breathe in and out as I watch my anger melt away.

I choose to ignore the anger of others.

I am learning to calm down and practise managing my anger.

I am learning to give myself emotional distance from tension and conflict.

ATTITUDE/ See Feelings also

I have a positive and healthy attitude today.

I'm changing my day by changing my attitude.

My feelings are my friends to-day.

I allow my feelings to change into positive energy today.

BALANCE

My life is in balance today.

I am balancing my personal, spiritual, and professional life today.

God is guiding me as I learn to live a well balanced life.

I take on just what I can handle.

I am learning to balance the demands on my life today.

I am learning to balance work and play.

I can learn to find balance in my life.

CAREER/See Job also

"It's kind of fun to do the impossible."
Walt Disney

I am moving forward in my career.

I'm finding the perfect career for me.
God is guiding me on my career path.

"I always knew that one day I would take this road but yesterday I did not know today would be the day."
Julia Cameron

CHANGES

"Blessed are the flexible,
for they shall not be bent out of shape."
Anon

CHANGES

I am worthy of positive changes in my life.

I am open to positive changes in my life today.

Nothing is stopping me from growing today!

I'm learning more quickly to recognize what I can not change.

I'm letting go of all my struggle to change what I can not change!

I am taking time to reflect, and enjoy the pleasure of new experiences.

I trust that I will know the right time to make changes in my life.

CHOICES/See Decisions

COMMITMENTS

I am fulfilling all my commitments

I keep all my promises today.

COMPASSIONATE

*The moment you think of the well being
of others, your mind widens
Dalai Lama*

COMPASSIONATE

> *"If you cannot be compassionate
> to yourself, you can not be
> compassionate to others."*
> *Thich Nhat Hanh*

I am a caring and compassion-
ate person.

I am a loving and compassion-
ate person today.

I am grateful for my compas-
sionate heart.

CONFIDENCE

Today I am fully alive, fully open
to feeling all that there is...knowing
that I can handle all that comes
my way.

I am a confident person today.

I am confident in my ability to meet challenges today.

I am a dynamic, confident, charismatic, motivating, fearless

_____

(Add your own word(s) here, i.e., speaker, leader, teacher, singer, writer, etc).

I have the confidence to express myself openly and freely today.

I have all that I need to do what is good and right in my life today.

I know that confidence grows with each success.

I am choosing to spend time with people who help me feel confident.

I am growing in self-confidence.

CONTROL

I'm letting go of my need to control everything.

I see my need to control as a block to me today and I am letting it go.

COURAGE

I wanted you to see what real courage is,
instead of getting the idea that courage is
a man with a gun in his hand.
It's when you know you're licked before
you begin but you begin anyway
and you see it through no matter what.
Harper Lee,
To Kill a Mockingbird

Change Almost Anything

COURAGE

My courage grows as I try new things.

The universe supports me as I push beyond my fear.

I have the courage of my convictions

I have all the courage I need to

_____

(Add your own word(s) here, i.e., take a plane ride, apply for a new job, speak up to my boss).

I have all the courage I need today to face my shortcomings.

CREATIVITY

Change Almost Anything

CREATIVITY

Today my creativity is flowing easily and effortlessly.

I am open to all the creativity of the universe.

God is showing me what a creative person I am.

DECISIONS

*"Everything is okay in the end. If it's not
okay, then it's not the end."*
                    Native American
                    Code of Ethics

decisions decisions decisions ???

DECISIONS

My Higher Power guides me in making healthy and positive decisions today.

I am being guided to make positive choices in my life today.

I am making healthy decisions today.

My decisions are positive and for the good of all concerned.

I choose healthy paths today.

I am at choice today.

I trust myself to make a good decision.

DIFFICULT SITUATION

difficult situation

Change Almost Anything

DIFFICULT SITUATIONS

*"The experience of life can become our
teachers; the accidental predicaments
of our lives are, in this sense,
spiritual opportunities."*
Tara Bennett-Goleman

I have all the strength, support
and guidance I need to get
through this situation.

I am willing to ask a friend to
help me through this situation.

I make things easy on myself
today.

God is guiding me through this
difficult time.

I can learn to ask for help when
things are tough.

ENERGY

I have all the energy I need to do everything that needs to be done today.

energy

ENERGY

All the positive energies of the universe are pouring through me today.

I choose to spend my energy in a balanced way.

My energy is a force for good in the world.

I use my energy to create positive results.

I am directing my energy in positive and loving ways.

I am open to all the positive and loving energies of the universe.

God gives me all the energy I need today to do all that needs to be done.

EXERCISE

My Higher Power gives me all the energy and incentive I need to exercise today.

I am taking good care of my body today.

I feel so good as I take time each day to exercise.

I weigh_____ (insert your intended realistic weight here) and I always have enough time, energy and desire to exercise my body.

I weigh_____(insert your intended, realistic weight here) and I have created my perfect body with slim, trim limbs and firm toned muscle.

FAITH

FAITH

My faith is increasing each day.

All the answers I need are coming to me as I need them.

I rely on my faith today.

I turn my will and my life over to the care of God today.

I put my faith in a power greater than myself.

I have faith that God is guiding me through this time.

Faith is fear that has said its prayers.

FAILURE

Failure is my path to success.

Failure is an opportunity for me to grow and to learn.

Failure spurs me to create positive outcomes today.

FAMILY/ See Friends and Relationships

FEAR

"Sooner or later we have to overcome our fears, because the spiritual path can only be traveled through the daily experience of love."

Paul Coelho

Change Almost Anything

FEAR

Fear can't stop me from moving forward.

Fear no longer owns me or is a threat to my day.

I'm letting go of my fear today.

I'm turning my fear into faith.

I am moving beyond my fear.

I am free of fear because I have faith.

FEELINGS

feelings... all kinds!

Change Almost Anything

FEELINGS

I am not my feelings.

It's okay to feel my feelings.

I do not have to act out on all my feelings.

I'm handling my feelings in a healthy way.

FINANCES

I am becoming debt-free to-day.

I am living within my means today

I am donating more freely to good causes.

All the money I need is flowing to me today.

My business is growing and prospering.

God is guiding me to use my money wisely.

I am financially responsible today.

I am contributing financially to the well being of others whenever possible.

I see money as a way of easing the pain of others.

Remember to feeeel the words as you say them

FOOD

God is guiding my food choices today.

FOOD/ See addictions and weight also

God is designing my menu today.

My food choices are healthy today.

I am eating what I need to stay healthy today.

Food is my friend today.

FORGIVENESS

I see my ability to forgive as a
gift from God.

free at last!

FORGIVENESS

I'm moving toward giving forgiveness today.

I'm letting go of all my
resentents today.

I accept forgiveness from others.

I am learning how to forgive
today.

I am willing to be a forgiving
person.

I am devoted to inner peace. I
forgive myself no matter what.

I let go of my judgments and
freely forgive.

FREEDOM

I am letting go of all my negativity and am becoming free to let joy into my life.

I am letting go of all the blocks that keep me stuck so I can be free to move forward.

I choose to be free today.

Today I trust that by searching deep withing for my own truth, I will discover the door to freedom and peace.

FRIENDS See Family and Relationships also

I take time for my friends today.

I am a good friend.

FUN

Change Almost Anything

FUN

I'm taking time to have fun today.

I give myself permission to play, explore, and create.

I take some time each day to laugh and play.

I spend at least a few minutes every day with loved ones just having fun.

GENEROSITY

"We make a living by what we get,
but we make a life by what we give."
Norman MacEswan

Change Almost Anything

GENEROSITY

I am growing in my ability to be generous.

I am able to share with others more freely.

I am a generous person!

I feel wonderful when I am able to give freely to others.

I am donating more freely to good causes.

I am more generous with my

_____

(Add your own words here, i.e., time, money, self).

I'm generous with my praise and compliments.

GOALS

My goals are for my highest good and for the highest good of all.

GOALS

I am setting realistic goals for me today.

My goals are positive and move me forward on a healthy path.

I am willing to set challenging goals for myself.

I am working a little every day to reach my goals.

GRIEF

Taking time to grieve brings relief from my pain.

grief... so heavy...

Change Almost Anything

GRIEF

I'm taking all the time I need to grieve.

Grieving is my path out of darkness.

GUIDANCE

All the energies of the universe are guiding me today.

God is guiding me on my path and my pace today.

I am being guided in positive directions today.

I pray for guidance in all that I do.

I am open to God's plan for me today.

HABITS

*"We are what we repeatedly do.
Excellence, then, is not an act, but a
habit."*
Aristotle

habits

HABITS

I am developing healthy habits today.

I am letting go of all the unhealthy habits that kept me stuck.

HARMONY

You don't get harmony when everybody
sings the same note.
Doug Floyd

harmony

HARMONY

I feel connected to the peace and harmony of the universe.

My life is flowing in harmony today.

My Higher Power is showing me how to remove all my blocks to peace and harmony.

*Remember to feeeel the words
as you say them*

HEALING/ HEALTH

Healing energy is flowing through all the cells of my body.

I feel vibrant and in good health.

Today I am connecting with my own natural rhythm and honoring it.

I am letting go of everything that threatens my health.

I am an instrument of God's healing love.

Healing energy is flowing through me with every breath I take.

I'm taking good care of my health today.

HONESTY

honesty

Change Almost Anything

HONESTY

I am living an honest life today.

I dare to tell the truth no matter what happens.

It feels so good to be truthful in all my affairs.

INDEPENDENCE

I am giving up my need to lean on others.

I am learning to be an interdependent person.

It's sometimes okay to need the help of others.

INSPIRATION

God gives me all the inspiration I need to have a wonderful day.

I feel inspired as I grow on my spiritual path.

I feel inspired to be the very best of who I am.

INTEGRITY

> *"If you have integrity,*
> *nothing else matters.*
> *If you don't have integrity,*
> *nothing else matters."*
> *Alan Simpson,*
> *former Senator*

I live with integrity today.

God guides me on a life filled with integrity.

Change Almost Anything

INTELLIGENCE

I have all the intelligence I need today to _____ (Add your own word(s) here, i.e., pass this test, do this job, write this book).

I am an intelligent person.

INTIMACY

I am opening myself to others.

I dare to be intimate today.

I am open to allowing others in today.

I'm letting myself be seen as I am.

INTUITION

I am learning to trust myself.

There is a special place within me where I find wisdom.

I trust the small voice inside of me.

*Remember to feeel the words
as you say them.*

JOB

*"But where is this going to lead me
to make me a more fully
realized person?"*
Nicole Kidman

JOB

God is guiding me to the perfect job for me today

I am perfect for this job.

I am in the process of getting the perfect job for me today.

I feel strong and confident in my job today!

I am working in a job that benefits people.

My work contributes to the good of humanity.

I am growing in my ability to do my job well.

JOY

JOY

I feel the joy of _____to-day. (Insert what is appropriate for you, i.e., teaching, running, parenting, skateboarding, writing, learning, etc).

I am open to having joy in my life.

I live joyfully.

I deserve joy today.

I feel the joy of living today.

I am finding time to have joy in my life.

JUDGEMENTS

I'm letting go of being judge-
mental today.

I am learning to live without
judging others.

I am accepting others as they
are.

As I practise letting go of my
judgements, all parts of me come
together and I feel complete.

LETTING GO

"We hold on so tightly that our hands are unavailable to reach out for the happiness we could gain by letting go."
M. J. Ryan

LETTING GO

But more frequently the task
is one of letting go,
of finding a gracious heart that
honors the changes in life.
                    Jack Kornfield

I'm leaving my work at work.

Today I am willing to let go of all anger and resentments that keep me stuck in tension and in pain.

My past no longer owns me.

I'm no longer a victim of my past.

I am letting go of

_____

(Insert your own intention here).

If we don't let go we can't move forward.

R.F.

Today I am willing to let go and let God work in my life.

I am letting go of all the negative thoughts that limit my choices.

I'm letting go of my self-imposed burdens today.

I'm letting go of my *shoulds* and *ought tos* today.

I'm letting go of my need to be perfect.

I'm letting go of my need to control everything.

LIFE

Just to be is a blessing.
Just to live is holy.
Rabbi Abraham Heschel

LIFE

I am open to new experiences today.

I am willing to live life on life's terms.

I love life today!

I choose to live my life in a positive way.

I am feeling passion in my life today!

I value life as a gift from God.

LOVE

*You come to love not by
finding the perfect person,
but by seeing an imperfect
person perfectly.*
        Sam Keen

LOVE

*The experience of love is a choice we make,
a mental decision to see love as the only real
purpose and value in any situation.*
                                   Marianne Williamson

Today I choose to see everyone through the eyes of love.

I am growing in love and compassion.

My heart is filled with love and compassion.

I can accept love today.

I choose to give love freely.

I am coming from a place of goodness and love today.

MEDITATION

The secret of meditation is to become conscious of each moment of your existence.

Thich Nhat Hahn

peace

MEDITATION

I am eager to meditate today.

I have all the time I need to meditate every day.

I am a daily meditator.

Meditation is a gift I lovingly give myself each day.

I release all my resistance and barriers to meditation today.

Meditation brings me closer to my Creative Source.

My meditation is flowing easily and effortlessly.

I feel myself filled with loving energy as I meditate today.

Change Almost Anything

MIRACLES

*Miracles are instantaneous, they cannot be
summoned, but come of themselves,
usually at unlikely moments and to those
who least expect them.*
                    Katherine Anne Porter

MIRACLES

I am open to all the miracles of this day.

I believe in miracles.

Today I have all the courage I need to let go of everything that is holding me back so that I can step forward and experience each miracle that is waiting for me.

I am clearing out old confusion and doubt so that I can see the miracles today.

MONEY/See finances

NEEDS

The universe is providing me with all my needs today.

All my needs are being met today.

I have everything I need today.

ORDER

There is Divine Order in my life today.

I am moving toward order and clarity.

I am clearing out the clutter of my life.

My life is full of peace and or-derliness.

PARENTING

My child/children is/are a great source of joy in my life.

I am willing to give my child/children the space he/she/they need when the time is right.

I am a calm, loving

_____
(Insert your own word here, i.e., parent, mother, father, guardian), filled with strength and flexibility, supporting my children in becoming all that they can be.

PEACE

*We look forward to the time when
the power of love will replace the love of
power. Then will the world know the
blessings of peace.*
William Ewart Gladstone

feels so good!

PEACE

I am taking the time today to do whatever I need to do to bring peace into my life.

I am feeling peace in this very moment.

I feel peace pouring through my entire body.

Peace and relaxation flow through me with every breath I take.

Peace is as close as my next breath.

I feel peace at all times.

I am positive and peaceful today.

I am filled with peace and har-mony.

I release the illusion of being rushed.

PERFECTIONISM

> *For only in the reality of our imperfection can we find the peace and serenity we crave."*
>
> *Ernest Kurst and Katherine Ketchum*

I'm letting go of my need to be perfect.

It feels so good to let go of per-fectionism as my goal.

I am looking for progress, not per-fection in my life.

PLANS/See goals also

*I always knew that one day I would take
this road but yesterday I did not know
today would be the day.*
                              Julia Cameron

I am planning my day to have
time to connect with God and me.

My plans for today are realistic
and manageable.

I look forward to God's guidance when I make my plans.

POSITIVE

Since my house burned down

I now have a better view

of the rising sun

Mathew Fox

positive

POSITIVE

I am positive and peaceful today.

I choose to have positive people in my life today.

I look for the positive in each situation.

Remember to *feeel* the words

PRAYER

Rise with the sun to pray.
Pray alone.
Pray often.
The Great Spirit will listen,
if you only speak.
Native American Code of Ethics

PRAYER

I take time to connect with my Higher Power every day.

I deepen my connection with God each day through prayer and meditation.

PRINCIPLES/ See Integrity and Values also

Lead your life so you won't be ashamed to sell the family parrot to the town gossip.
Anon

I live a life based on principles today.

I trust my innersense of what is right for me.

PROCRASTINATION/ See Time also

Even if you're on the right track,
you'll get run over if you just sit there.
Will Rogers

I do what needs to be done
when it needs to be done.

I do things immediately today.

I do things today so I will have
more time tomorrow.

PURPOSE

Let the beauty you love be what you do.
There are a thousand ways to kneel and
kiss the earth.
-Rumi

Change Almost Anything

PURPOSE/also see Guidance and Job

> *To find our calling is to find the*
> *intersection between our own deep*
> *gladness and the world's deep hunger.*
> *Frederick Buechner*

I am positive and directed and have purpose in my life.

My next step is becoming clear

I am waiting patiently for clarity of my purpose.

RELATIONSHIPS

The experience of love is a choice we make,
a mental decision to see love as the only real
purpose and value in any situation.
                              Marianne Williamson

RELATIONSHIPS/See Family and Friends also

Today I am finding the good in all the people to whom I am connected.

I am willing to live in the present moment and not continue to go over regrets and resentments of the past.

Today I am willing to accept people as they are, not as I would like them to be.

I am finding the perfect partner for me today.

The universe is guiding me to the perfect partner for me.

God is guiding me into a healthy relationship

I am meeting a healthy, positive and available person

I am attracting positive people in my life today.

I am attracted to positive and loving people and positive and loving people are attracted to me.

I am a loving _____ (Insert your own word here, i.e., partner, friend, parent, daughter, son, lover, grandmother).

I am a positive and loving person.

I value the role of others in my life today.

I am learning to love without judgement today.

I am happy for the success of others.

I am happy to be one among many today.

I surround myself with positive and healthy people today.

RELAXATION

Change Almost Anything

RELAXATION/see School-Related
also

I am leaving my work at work.

I am taking time for me today!

I feel relaxed and calm today.

I am learning to relax today.

I deserve to take time for me today.

RESENTMENTS

Avoid hurting the hearts of others. The poison of your pain will return to you.
Native American
Code of Ethics

RESENTMENTS/ see Letting Go also

I am willing to let go of all the resentments today that are keeping me stuck in the past.

RESPECT

If I take five minutes out of each day to remember to treat others the way I want to be treated, we could accomplish wonderful things together.

Bob Fishel

I am respected in my profession, and what the universe offers me today reflects that.

I deserve to be treated with respect.

I respect and care for my body today.

I treat others with respect.

I respect the differences in people.

Remember to *feeel* the words

RESPONSIBILITY

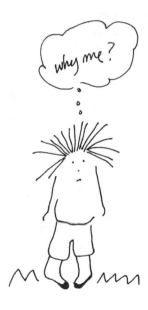

RESPONSIBILITY

I take full responsibility for my life today.

I am responsible for the results of my words and actions.

Today I am responsible for myself and I let others be responsible for themselves.

I am responsible, organized, motivated and productive today.

SAFETY

I am safe today.

I find safety with my friends and family.

God is keeping me safe.

SCHOOL-RELATED

graduation day

SCHOOL-RELATED/See Relaxation
also

   I am passing my exams with
ease.

   I am passing my course with
ease

   I am filled with all the knowledge I need to pass this test.

   I am passing my exam with
flying colors.

   My mind is relaxed and open to
all that I need to learn today.

   I am focused on my studies.

   I get all my homework in on
time.

   I am a terrific student!

I am finding learning to be fun and exciting.

I am doing the very best I can.

I'm becoming smarter and smarter every day.

I am learning to refrain from judging myself if I have trouble with

_____

(Insert your own word here, i.e., reading, spelling, speaking, writing, typing, computers, etc).

I am learning to refrain from demeaning myself if something is too hard. I can ask for help without feeling less than others.

SELF-CONFIDENCE/ see Confidence and Self-Esteem also.

I am growing in self-confidence.

SELF-ESTEEM/ See Self-confidence and Confidence also.

"The 'self-image' is the key to human personality. Change the self-image and you change the personality and the behavior."
Maxwell Maltz, M.D.,F.I.C.S.

I am terrific just the way I am!

I am respected in my profession, and what the universe offers me today reflects that.

I believe in myself today.

I deserve to be treated with love and respect.

I am good enough just the way I am.

Today I dare to be with me and all that I am.

Today I treat myself as my own best friend with gentleness and love.

I value myself today.

My ego is fed in healthy ways.

I celebrate my strengths, abilities and talents.

SELF PITY

Change Almost Anything

SELP-PITY

I am giving up my need for self-pity today.

I am finding healthy ways to feel good about myself.

God is replacing my self-pity with gratitude.

There is always a place where I can go and find safety.

God is guiding me safely on my journey.

SHAME

I am letting go of the burden of shame in my life.

My past no longer owns me.

SIMPLICITY

Change Almost Anything

SIMPLICITY

I'm keeping my life simple today.

God is guiding me in a simple life today.

I'm learning to simply be.

SOLITUDE/ See Time also

I welcome the peace, serenity, wisdom, and spirituality I find when I take time for solitude.

Everyone can do without me while I take some time for solitude.

It is important that I take time alone to connect with God each day.

I deserve some special time in solitude.

SPIRITUALITY

Affirmations such as
'I am a child of the universe,'
and 'God takes care of injustice,' or
'I am safe and I trust God's justice,'
turn us in the right direection.
                                    Barbara Berger

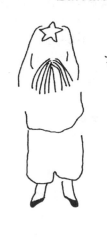

SPIRITUALITY/ See Prayer also

Allow God to speak through you
and smile upon the earth through you,
because you are an unconditional giver, a
purposeful being.
                                        Dr. Wayne Dyer

I am growing toward others and God today.

God is guiding me on my spiritual path to recovery.

My spirituality is deepening as I take time to pray and meditate each day.

I am growing as a spiritual human being.

I am one with god.

STRUGGLE

I am given up my need to struggle.

I am willing to move forward, in spite of my struggles.

struggle

Change Almost Anything

SUCCESS

I am successful in all that I do today.

God is guiding me forward successfully.

I am working toward successful results.

My relationships are successful today.

SUFFERING

I've outgrown the need to suffer.
12 Step Expression

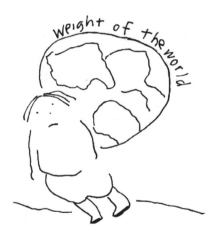

Change Almost Anything

SURRENDER

I surrender the things that hold me back.

I can't. God can. I think I'll let God.

I give up my need to do everything alone.

TALENTS

Change Almost Anything

TALENTS

Use what talents you possess; the woods would be very silent if no birds sang except those that sang best.

Henry Van Dyke

I am so grateful for my God-given talents.

I'm developing my God-given talents.

My talents and abilities are valued and needed, and what the universe offers me today reflects that.

TEACHING

I feel the joy of teaching today!

Change Almost Anything

TEACHING/ See School-Related also

I am a confident, encouraging and motivating teacher.

I am grateful for the gift of being able to contribute to the lives of my students.

I feel the joy and enthusiasm that brought me to this profession.

Even though it is not always obvious, my teaching is changing the lives of many of my students.

If there is one student I can help, my day is worth while

TIME

on time.
my time.

TIME/ See Procrastination and Solitude also

I'm doing everything on time today.

I have all the time I need to do everything that is good and right in my life today.

I'm taking time for me today.

TODAY

I'm living my life one day at a time.

My past no longer owns me.

I have put aside my regrets from the past and fear of the future.

I can do anything for one day.

This is the first day of the rest of my life.

TRAFFIC

I am flexible; I am calm; I am forgiving; I have plenty of time!

I am relaxed and patient.

I am arriving at the perfect time.

I am enjoying this extra time to relax.

TRAVEL

God is guiding me safely home.

I am traveling safely.

God is in charge of my trip.

TRUST

trust

TRUST

I'm learning to trust my instincts today.

I'm trusting_____
(Insert your own word(s) here, i.e., God, myself, others, people I love, people who care about me).

I'm trusting that my intentions are coming from good and love.

VALUES/see Principles and Integrity also

I take time to recognize my core values.

I am living my life, consistent with my values.

WEIGHT/ See addictions and food also

I am in the process of arriving at a healthy weight for me.

I am proud to be eating correctly today.

My Higher Power is guiding me to eat healthy and lose weight.

I weigh _____(Put in your own intended, realistic weight) and I maintain my weight easily, eating foods that are healthy and consistent with a slim, trim figure.

WILLINGNESS

I am willing to do everything I can to nurture my body, mind and soul.

I am willing to be a positive and loving person.

God gives me all the willingness I need to grow as a spiritual human being.

I am willing to do everything that is good and right today.

I am willing to be willing to

_____

(Put your own intention here, i.e., give up sweets, walk one mile daily, study for my exams).

I can do anything for one day.

WORLD PEACE

WORLD PEACE

I take time each day to pray for world peace.

I know I am making a positive difference in the world today.

Today I am being a lttle kinder to everyone I meet.

Today I will be my very best to bring peace to my life and to the lives of those around me.

I am sending thoughts of peace and love to my world family today.

MY PERSONAL 21 DAY JOURNAL

Here are 21 pages for your first affirmation. Choose one change you would like to make in your life and begin now!

Remember, they must be
1. **POSITIVE**
2. Said and felt with **PASSION** and **POWER**
3. Be in the **PRESENT** moment
4. **POSSIBLE**
5. **PERSONAL**

Please don't be too hard on yourself if you miss a day. If you find that you have skipped a day, just start over again with day one.

Whether you are consciously aware of it or not, your affirmations are working for you.

As you write your affirmations, know that you are in the process of becoming the author of your own life script!

Congratulations!

Day One

*I have all the energy and willingness to write
my affirmation ten times today.*

Thank You

Change Almost Anything

Day Two

All the energies of the universe are working
for my affirmation today.

Thank You

Day Three

***Everything is flowing easily and effortlessly
in my life today.***

Thank You

Change Almost Anything

Day Three

I can feeeel positive changes happening in my life today

Thank You

Day Five

Positive energy flows through me as I grow on my spiritual path toward love and peace.

Thank You

Change Almost Anything

Day Six

My Higher Power is working in my life today.

Thank You

Day Seven

I have new strength and purpose as I continue to write my affirmations

Thank You

Change Almost Anything

Day Eight

Positive changes are already happening as I write my affirmations today

Thank You

Day Nine

It is powerful to know that I do not make my changes alone

Thank You

Day Ten

I am grateful that affirmations work in my life

Thank You

Day Eleven

I feeeel my affirmation happening with every part of my body and my mind and my spirit.

Thank You

Change Almost Anything

Day Twelve

As I go through this day I know that my Higher Power is guiding me.

Thank You

Day Thirteen

It is exciting to know that my life is moving in a positive and healing direction.

Thank You

Day Fourteen

I am in the process of releasing all my resistance and doubts and fears so that my affirmation can work in my life today.

Thank You

Day Fifteen

Everything is happening for goodness and love.

Thank You

Change Almost Anything

Day Sixteen

I am doing the footwork today.

Thank You

Day Seventeen

*My Higher Power is guiding me on my path
and my pace today.*

Thank You

Change Almost Anything

Day Eighteen

*My purpose for this day is to become more
and more clear as I write my affirmations*

Thank You

Day Nineteen

I have all the energy that I need to do that which is good and right in my life.

Thank You

Day Twenty

I am the author of my own
life script today.

Thank You

Day Twenty One

I am writing my affirmation ten times a day for twenty one days.

Thank You

Change Almost Anything

Notes

Notes

Change Almost Anything

INDEX

Change Almost Anything

ABOUT THE AUTHOR

Ruth Fishel is an author, speaker, national trainer and workshop leader.She has been teaching programs of inspiration and spirituality to people for over 20 years.

Ruth is currently teaching **STOP! DO YOU KNOW YOU'RE BREATHING?,** a program she developed for teachers and students to help them deal with stress, addictions, anger and violence. **STOP!** also helps to improve performance on tests such as the MCAS

Call Spirithaven or email to be put on the mailing list, sign up for workshops and retreats, or have Ruth come to your school or business.

508-420-5301

EMail: spirithaven@spirithaven.com

Visit us on the web at:
www.Spirithaven.com

Other books by Ruth Fishel

Hang in 'til the Miracle Happens (6.95)
Precious Solitude ($10.95)
The Journey Within: A Spiritual Path to Recovery ($8.95)
Time for Joy: Daily Affirmations ($6.95)
Time for Thoughtfulness ($7.95)
Take Time for Yourself ($8.95)
STOP! Do You Know You're Breathing?
   A Guide for Teachers and Parents ($13.95)

Tapes ($10.00 each):
You Can't Meditate Wrong
The Journey Within
Deepening Your Meditation
Transforming Your Past into Presents
Time for Joy
Discovering Your Source of Peace

Books and Tapes are available at your
local bookstore or at Spirithaven
17 Pond Meadow Drive
Marstons Mills, MA 02648
508-420-5301
EMail: spirithaven@spirithaven.com
Visit us on the web at
www.Spirithaven.com